Deliberate
and
Accidental
Acts

DELIBERATE AND ACCIDENTAL ACTS

poems
by
Thomas
Zvi
Wilson

Bk Mk Press
University of Missouri–Kansas City

ACKNOWLEDGMENTS

"Solo" appeared as a visual poem in *Stiletto II.*

Earlier versions of "Answering the Knock," "During the
Angiogram," "Solo," "Stone Hearth and Chimney
Three Miles East of Hope, Arkansas," "The Leatherback,"
"Rabbit Fox Owl Crow," "Baxter Township Jail, 1933,"
"Season Ticket Holder," "*Aholibah Catocala,*"
"Five Clay Pieces from Zaire," "The *Golem,*" "Shanghai Sally,"
"What I Did on My Summer Vacation in Brooklyn,"
and "*Arthur Bryant's Barbeque*" were included in the author's
audio collection, *Things That Are Not,* which he aired
on KKFI-FM's *Contemporary Issues in the Arts,*
produced and edited by Jim Leedy.

Cover and book designs by author.

Library of Congress Cataloging-in-Publication Data

Wilson, Thomas Zvi, 1931-
   Deliberate and accidental acts / Thomas Zvi Wilson.
     p. cm.
   Poems.
   ISBN 1-886157-10-3
   I. Title.
PS3573.I47537D4 1997
811'.54--dc21   96-36894
                                  CIP

In the cold light of reason,
poetry is impossible to write.
CHARLES SIMIC

I

—

II

—

—

III

―
―
―

IV

―
―
―
―

for Jeanie

ANSWERING THE KNOCK

The poet answers the knock,
throws open the door to welcome the muse.
It's the landlord screaming for rent;
a wife from years ago, cursing;
the man in a dingy suit
who collects unpaid bills for half
the merchants on the street.

Again and again the poet
jumps up from his chair,
drags wet from his bath,
leaps from between a lover's legs,
or rushes with tomato soup
smeared across his chin
to answer the knock,
till he sees *Death* slouched on the sill,
humming a familiar tune.

ROSTER

This death is bought with mangos,
that one with roasted pigs.
Some are quiet, some loud.
This one repeats itself
like pain. This death,
ecstasy; that one, defeat.
One by fire, one by sword;
two from love,
three from neglect.
A babe followed by
a twisted, old man.
A woman in her prime;
a muddied, bloodied PFC.
Cain follows Abel,
followed by all the *begets,*
the Son of God,
the lamb.
Mozart, Rasputin, Dachau;
the neighbor to the left.
Next.

DURING THE ANGIOGRAM

He runs home movies in reverse, watches

his kids scream down a roller coaster,
paint their rowboat blue,
blow out candles, shred gift wrap
as if they were tornadoes,
till Johnny disembodies, Peggy's voice stills;
then the Poconos honeymoon cottage
and heart-shaped pool slide off screen
with Roz and him.

His teen years unwind on sprockets into childhood:
neighbors speckle the screen,
along with his Gramps, Aunt Lilly,
Dad before he lost his arm,
Mom without the facial tick.

In slept-in khakis,
his brother Billy limps off the *Greyhound;*
pimpled classmates grin or grimace,
Troop 7 bantams poke each other
at a powwow in Muncie Park;
faces smooth out squints,
swallow smiles, gulp laughter,
pop words back, fade out of sight.

1 / 9

Flipping backwards through the family album,

the twins wave, board planes for Berkeley and Purdue;
their names crowd each other on birthday cakes;
they bounce rubber balls off the stoop
on the green stuccoed house on Mercer Street;
his coached smiles masquerade wedding nerves
from force-fed cake to aisle parade;
his flowing robe at Notre Dame
covers blue-gold gym shorts;
buddies elbow him on the corner playground,
after softball and soccer games.

Snapshots of Saturday backyard barbecues
show his father squinching
through bent-framed glasses,
his mom wearing her weekly crown
of turquoise curlers.

He leafs pages till he can't speak, can't crawl;
the breast is sun and moon,
his dimpled ass, bare on the rug.

BOOK REVIEW

Pablo Picasso's painting,
"The Bathers" (c. 1918),
is reproduced on the cover
of "Rapture" by Susan Mitchell

Here's *Rapture,*
just the book
for the girls of summer;

pink-tipped on tiptoe,
they turn to the sun,
twist truth into beauty.

In this book is crammed:
leaves unfurling,
meant to be plucked;

promises like
ripe peaches pitted, purged
of anything pointed, obstinate;

pages that layer
buds of blood, crimson
with life's denial and bait.

Closed, it holds
secrets
death whispers.

SELECTED POEMS

The thick, textured paper tells you
she's an important poet,
walks on air, walks on water,
teaches at Wesleyan,
Guggenheim Fellowship, National
Book Critics Award,
two husbands, one mastectomy.
Each page
screams obscenities;
cannot stop.

Her hymen somehow still intact,
page fourteen blossoms blood.
On the flip side,
she is raped but barely satisfied
that it was worth the droll sestina.
Cream tinted pages tell
how her father died, and by which hand;
how her mother lit candles six days a week,
drank herself into Sabbath stupors.
Her mother's twisting. No one's counting.
She's found hanging, a man's technique.

The book winds through two wars, three
European capitals, eight cities stateside.
Everyone is dying, dead.
Each day clouds hang like black shawls,
the uniform of widows in Sicily, in Crete.
Someone's sucked the laughter from her lines.
Even the ink is black.

1 / 12

JOB

A beaver lives inside his brain.
Eels swim in the chambers of his heart.
Blind, newborn mice
suckle polyps in his lungs.
From his throat to his anus
a convoluted serpent stretches.

Job dreams the worm
turning him.

REVELATION 666

The books have never balanced.
His 120mm head is bald,
his casing is spinning.
A word fired at random
catapults him to hell –
a free fall tumble down the shell
of the Sears Tower; the Autobahn
at 200 kilometers an hour,
in a Ferrari on fire.

His world's a jaybird,
joke, jellyfish,
naked in orbit.

SOLO

Ben told me,
Everything in my world pitches and yaws:
desks, pencils, trucks,
buildings, bicycles.
Only the earth stands still.

All his life Ben felt awash.
He swerved round capsized
hydrants, bridges, telephone poles,
careening as if pounded by tidal waves.
At the zoo, rhinos, camels, people tumbled.
His office listed, its moorings
always loosed. Bedeviled even at home,
he dodged storm-battered chairs, frying pans.

At thirty-three
he dove from his high-rise window,
plunged to the pavement anchored below.

THE GLUTTON

He staggers from the table
like a wounded rhino;
topples over with a bellyful of pain.

They hoist him through a grimy window
like a grand piano, build
his casket with wood for three,

and shake their heads, never understanding
his every bite held love at bay,
the only way he knew.

MONEY ORDER

The knife thrower
promised her 200 bucks
for any miss below the neck,
fifty extra for a cut
on the face;
otherwise a thousand
to her mother in El Dorado.

STONE HEARTH AND CHIMNEY
THREE MILES EAST OF HOPE, ARKANSAS

I knew all six of the Birdsalls:
Jethrop and his jug;
Becky Mae, pinched round her bones;

the little ones, stacked like stairs,
who huddled with their bruises
under dirty quilts.

One set the fire while the others slept.
One said, *Set us free, Lord.*
Hallelujah.

THE LEATHERBACK

He draws
half-a-ton across the sand,
mistakes a puffed-out plastic lunch bag
for jellyfish
or man-of-war.

RABBIT
FOX
OWL
CROW

In a burst of need,
rabbit scent hurls fox
into a trap of triggered teeth.

Fox sacrifices self for self,
chews through leg,
licks blood,
dances away a three-legged jig
till owl shows fox how to fly.

Bullet breaks owl's grip,
plunges fox like stone
into bed of leaves

where, twisting into himself,
he stains the snow
that saves fox for crow.

BAXTER TOWNSHIP JAIL, 1933

He told the man who came
from Riverton to translate
how he happened to marry his second wife,
how he pounded a spike
into her forehead to stop the snoring.

In Polish he explained, *Milking*
needs a steady hand
before the sun is even up.

That night they found him dangling,
blood on his forehead squeezed from his wrist.

AUGUST AFTERNOON
IN STONE COUNTY, ARKANSAS

Three men squat in a circle
by the side of a tar paper shack;
two voices low to the ground
like crickets.

One spits to the side.
One rubs his thigh and knee.

They stand,
and the one who failed to speak
pulls a pistol from his pocket,
with two shots kills the others.

A hawk startles, flies on.
A dog goes back to sleep.

AT THE *PIZZA PARLOR*

When he woke he knew.
His 12 gauge said, *I do,*

at the *Pizza Parlor,*
all you can eat, at noon;

the shells cool, smooth
as skin before sex.

At 12:05 his lips tasted
the hollow muzzle.

WEATHER REPORT

I

The Alabama night is wild
with the twang of saplings,
shrieks in silhouetted trees.
A twister in your eye bangs
trailers together like cymbals.

II

Seventy sunny degrees,
thunderclaps,
big guns on battleships
bombard San Diego suburbs.

III

We swing to Camera Three,
the satellite picture,
the pointer,
the temperature in Hays, Kansas.

THE WARSAW GHETTO SURVIVOR, 1944

In the concrete playground
beneath the elevated *BMT*
Broadway-Canarsie line,
between monkey bars and slides,
near seesaws and swings,
he tipped back his head, gulped down
three bottles of drugstore iodine, fell
thrashing like a headless chicken,
screaming the *Shema,*
leaving nothing for the ambulance
but dead weight and a name.

His body harvested, sirens silenced,
the children plunged into play
with laughter, ferocity.

SEASON TICKET HOLDER

She wore black to every concert.
From her clothes she plucked
lint, threads, specks
like pizzicato notes.

Hair scissored close to skull
laid bare neck and profile.
She'd pinched the smile from her face,
scrubbed her joints free of grace.
European, I guessed, probably German.

Tonight, she's on the late news.
Her bony wrist, tattooed with ciphers,
steadies her daughter's hand that lights
candles for victims of Auschwitz.

The anchorman describes a fire,
the weatherman reads rain in radar.
The sportscaster shuffles numbers.
I check the doors.

DANCING WITH THE *WORD*

Sewn strips of parchment,
wound on spindles like bandages,
heal the Holocaust,
pogroms, purges,
exiles and sacrileges.
Jews call them *Torahs*.

On *Simchat Torah* they take
the scrolls from the arks,
clutch them, dance
all day with the *Word,*
put the lie to death.

ELLIPTIC MOON
MARCH 8, 1993

Nearer than the jar of jam,
the butcher knife, the almanac,
the man in the moon is old, pinched,
never suffers lovers,
makes no sense, has no reason.
The books he buries, he read backward.
The songs he sings are upside down.
He has no teeth yet plucks
owls from the night.

Craters and debris
mark his elliptic moon
that charms the living
and visits the dead.
When the sun spits,
he slides silent into himself.

GRAFFITI: A STRATEGY

Spray paint is for kids.
He doodles with gasoline;
scurries off the Interstate, searching
for wooden churches, hay-stuffed barns, towns
with silos and shanties near railroad sidings.
He torches his signature until
its mouth swallows its tail.

He lights up the night,
runs like hell, turns to watch,
to contemplate Nero's deed;
sighs deeply as he daydreams Manhattan,
Maine forests, the world burning,
glowing in his fireplace on Christmas Eve.

Now the sun is rising, a focused fire.
Time to set down his five gallon can
till Night cries out in darkness.

SWALLOWING THE NIGHT

She told him once
what the sun did.
He believed her
the night she caught
the moon in a net,
drew two ears, two eyes,
tacked on a tail,
made it a mouse,
a funny, sad mouse,
and swallowed it.

AHNALOOWAH'S OFFERING

She carries a bowl of clay
she kneaded, molded into a jaguar,
incised with serpent and diamond shapes,
then fired for seven days, seven nights.

Into it she pours trickles from a spring,
sprinkles blood,
spoons menstrual clots,
floats three leaves
from the crawa bush –
stirs the sacred drink called *chimooah*
by the women of her people.

She brings the jaguar bowl
to the granite cliff,
nests it in tangled roots
at the foot of the wabooah tree.

The condor will lift it,
raise it to the god who has
so many names he has none,
the god of darkness.
From his bowels
the sun will drop.

IN DRY, WIDE SPACES

In dry, wide spaces,
the sun pokes out
from night's navel.

Cardinal out of crow,
sun births itself,
purifies itself with fire.

This chameleon, burst
from flat lines,
scattered hills,

blots out the moon,
climbs the minutes until
white light blinds it.

PRISONER

In his cell, four feet by seven,
he is father, brother, son.
They share the three-legged stool,
cot slung from concrete wall,
seatless commode.

Each night they pass around
bits of day like smoldering butts.
Come morning, they yawn, blink.
To steel's clatter
they shuffle into day.

AHOLIBAH CATOCALA

for Virginia Woolf

The *aholibah catocala* moth
folds back wings from sight,
clings with tibial spurred legs
to the window screen's ripped
and rusted weather side.

It landed in a stain of glare
where there's shade now.
A cold wind strokes its wings.

THE SUN KILLER

A killer's hangin' round
behind that mountain there.
Every day, 'bout this time,
he snares the sun,
pulls her down
an' strangles her.
No one's catched him –
not never.

But hang around a while,
and a new sun's born,
over in that valley.
It stretches, rises
like a redbird hatched, fed,
and chased from the nest,
when the time's right.

But wait.
Wait.
That ol' killer's
still hangin' round.

TEN FINGERS LAKE

The dam built, the lake
searched its level for twelve years,
stretched out its coves for fingers.

It drowned trees, houses,
Grover Cleveland School,
the Brethren and Baptist churches;
covered fields and towns
with an everlasting shroud.

Graves gave up their dead and markers,
pastures their livestock,
woods their mice and deer.

Where cars once sliced the valley,
catfish meditate.

CAREFUL WHEN DRIVING IN THE DARK

Along rain-glossed highways
to Fargo, Shreveport, Walla Walla,
tire-etched, bloodied coons
come back to life to carve
the roadbeds, drag them into night.

Cars lose their way, skid,
slide into weed-grown ditches.
Soon weasels, possums, wild dogs
rip out bright lights,
drag off grills, skin back hoods,
tear out cylinders from baked, hot hearts.

Moonless nights, you can hear them
in gravel pits, cattail clumps,
below the bridges –
dividing booty, digging
shallow graves for bones.

CITY LIGHTS

10:00 A.M.
From my hotel room, thirty stories high,
I watch Lilliputians on a slant roof
crawl like circus clowns
up crazy, tilted scaffolds.
If they slip they'll plunge
10,000 miles, slam into asphalt.

9:00 P.M.
Almost everything man-made
angles to meet itself.
Office lights move on checkerboards,
reflect off gloves of glass
skinned over shafts that climb
to mythic moonlight, displacing air.
Skyscraper roofs flicker red
to ward off planes that slice the night.

3:00 A.M.
It is slick, stick cold tonight.
Nuns and defrocked bishops
twist in darkness, clinking beads.
In the cookie cutter Loop, Baptists, Jews,
and Sikhs stare through jaundiced eyes.
Death feeds in cubbyholes below.

Field, Adler, Navy Pier,
Chicago River, death-dark.
A jumper's paradise, the city
of Polacks, jazz, Marshall Field,
Water Tower and Carson Pirie Scott cries out:
Is this London, 1356?
Is this darkness the plague?

Votive lighthouse flashes red its stations.
Lightning strikes the set on cue.

EACH SMALL BONE

One at a time he fashions
each small bone,
each tight sinew,
each ligament.
He spends days
carving her jaw,
sanding down her brow.
Her throat he tunes
with wire thin as truth;
turns each breast
on a tender lathe.
The feet take forever.

FIVE CLAY PIECES FROM ZAIRE

A black *mulondo* from Lunda
The pitcher is modeled after a warrior
to hold safe his spirit.
His right hand forms the handle,
his left hand grips a snake.
His lips are clenched to stop the snake
from sliding into his mouth;
swallowing his spirit;
crawling out his anus,
leaving his insides black.

A bottle from Teke
Shoulder scored zig-zag in the round,
its fired clay steals leather's look.
Slender as a virgin,
the neck rises, flares.

A triple-spouted jar from Bale
Smooth as riverbed rock, black as earth,
its thong is braided antelope hide.
Its spirits tell
from which mouth to drink.

An incised bowl from Tabwa
The *Rising of the New Moon* pattern
is named *Balamwezi.*
The new moon falls into the concave bottom,
reflects faces, drinks them in.

A vessel from Muba
The color of skin, its walls are forty
centimeters high, thin as membranes.
It is oval as a woman full
of children pushing toward the moon.
The potter perched her head,
bent like a branch,
forced out her soul.

THE *GOLEM*

The *golem* is a bundle of fused nerves,
a bagful of secondhand bones,
beakers of siphoned blood.
His cranium resounds with electric jolts
and borrowed memories that grate.
Stitched together from a *minyan* of cadavers,
a messenger from the other side,
he pulsates man-made time.

Moving from grace
the way we hurry from horror,
he cannot comprehend the sin
of his maker's triumph over death.
The *golem* harbors darkness.
He never knew a womb.
The hands that fashioned him
loved him not.

MR. RIGHT

You had almost given up hope on finding Mr. Right
when there he was...
"Marilyn Monroe Meets the Creature
from the Black Lagoon"
CATHERINE N. PARKE

The creature from the Black Lagoon
stretches his six feet of chlorinated musk
on the black silk sheets beside his Marilyn,
checks his erection for seaweed strands,
turns full-length to her and gurgles valentines.

The goddess of the flicks, as slick
as porpoise, shark or shelled shrimp,
spreads her lips with secret promise,
swirls down to darkness with him,
drinks him in.

When they find her
there's no trace of him; no hide, no hair,
not one amphibious limb. He remains
a fantasy too far left of beaded silver screen;
far too right to live on freeze-framed
even in her shadows.

But now, Kennedy too is gone and half her fans,
co-stars stripped to bones,
stills and film faded, theaters torn down.

And the Creature from the Black Lagoon?
Back at Loch Ness, far from sonic sound,
he dodges tourists, cameras,
and the curious metaphor.

SHANGHAI SALLY

She worked the tattoo
on her stomach like a puppet;
had it do things
their mothers never dreamt;
things they first learned
on liberty in Luzon.

Then she lifted a silver dollar
from a table on the stage
with two lips moist
between her thighs.

When they filed out,
she was waiting by the back door
for the boys from the *Arizona.*

She wasn't easy to forget
until the seventh of December.

KANDINSKY

Lines escape their origins.
Circles end where they began.
Pelvic bones of triangles part,
converge, articulating tension.

Equal are the means by which
objects fulfill forms,
defining objects.

Everything more than it is,
less than it could be,
his pigments prove
whatever's possible is art.

Each thing captured
he set free.

SEVEN FOR THE WEEK

... the earth was without form ...
GENESIS 1:2

CIRCLE
True to center, it can shrink or swell.
Role cast by whole, its perimeter
has zero points of departure or return.
A gentled square with formula of pi,
it harbors straight-edged wedges.

STRIPE
It requires a deliberate or accidental act.
Traveling in alternate directions,
a stripe begins at a point
prior to which it existed
invisibly or not at all.
Unless layered,
it divides what it is not.

Left open or closed,
a stripe shapes form when angled or curved.
Each side suggests a choice.
Add one dimension, and what began
humble is ready for breath of life,
its place in *Genesis.*

TRIANGLE
Right angled,
its hypotenuse defines it,
whereas equidistant pinnacles
thrice provide its proof.
Even nailed to the page, it moves.

SQUARE
Cursed with redundancy,
squarely divisible into squares,
a square's only opportunity
for variance is size.

RHOMBOID

Rectangle tipped oblique
to askew degrees, causes
its kind to be categorized
by special noun from French.
Its corners are obtuse
elbows and knees which crease
to delineate the oddly
structured space within.

OCTAGON

Eloquent even in silence,
more symmetrical than a womb,
an octagon embraces itself.
A barn in Pennsylvania or Virginia,
a garden flagstone, a tile trivet,
but never a different form.

OVAL

Circle push-pulled by cosmic forces
top to bottom, side to side,
into asymmetry invested with
beginnings struggling to be born.

CIRCLE

In three dimensions a sphere, a globe:
world, sun and moon tumbling
through day, through night,
falling only to rise.

Curvaceous cousin of cycle,
circle holds our lives and all
that comes round again.

HOMAGE TO MAGRITTE

These letters
                  words
                                lines
                                              float on the page.

The page is a cloud
that

      d

          e

               s

            c

                e

                     n

                            d

                                  s

                                      from the sky.

                DON'T BE ALARMED
                   when it turns
                   into a homburg,
                an apple or a pipe.

           Ceci n'est pas une poeme.

THE POET'S PLAN

... the word or two
that has to be said.
WALT WHITMAN

Like lust, the poem
starts up in his head, shakes out
in his eager hand.

Then he moves each word
across the page,
castles for the sake
of simpler syntax,
removes a word
as king takes pawn,
sacrifices a line
for a strophe's strategy.

His concern:
not word, not line,
nor single stanza.
His long range plan:
to win the page.

ENDINGS

Abuse of language is a fatal step.
C.W. GUSEWELLE

First the books rend their bindings,
then burn their endpapers for ashes
to attend their grief.
Pages disperse.
Paragraphs tumble and scatter.
Sentences come unglued.
Words fall to earth.
Letters fragment into shards.
Entire libraries bleed their punctuation.
Meanings turn to doubts, then to dust.
Language dies.
Nothing remains
from which to fashion eulogies.

Without words tongues stick,
minds shudder,
lovers cannot know each other;
mothers, fathers become
strangers to their children.
Curses pass unuttered, psalms unsung.
Everyone's in solitude.
Each brain can hardly speak to itself.
Dreams abort.
Rats eat intentions.
Everything caves in.
Earth falls out of sky
silently as snow.
The sun shuts down.

IV

WHAT I DID ON MY SUMMER VACATION IN BROOKLYN

In 1938,
the summer of a caterpillar plague,
I stole Heshy's three-ring binder,
ripped out its hardware.

On the concrete sidewalk I slaughtered larvae,
clamping them in shiny, snapping jaws
in front of Poppa's laundry store.

That was when I learned
to lie and steal,
and count up to a hundred.

POPPA FELL WHEN I WAS SIX

He once said to me, *Anger makes me stronger,* but
three days ago he clutched his chest, fell to the floor.
The doctor came, shook my hand.
No one had shook my hand before.

Yesterday, Aunt Rivkah yelled at me, *Herschel,*
if you stop reading Psalms, your poppa will die,
so now I skip around from psalm to psalm.
In death there is no remembrance of Thee;
In the nether-world who will give Thee thanks?

Hannah, my oldest sister, tiptoes into the damp,
shade-drawn room, lays her hand on my neck.
Last Saturday, this room was drowned in sunlight,
and Hannah played *Red-Light-Green-Light*
and *Simon Says* with me.
I'd had a hacking cough and Momma told me
I didn't have to go to *shul.*
Again! Poppa mumbled, slammed the door.

O, Lord my god; Lighten my eyes,
lest I sleep the sleep of death.
Soon I'll know half the psalms by heart.

Poppa, what other cheder boy can read
Hebrew good as me?
When you get well, ask me to peel your apple;
teach me how the chess horse jumps,
what it means to castle.

HANNAH, MY OLDEST SISTER

Momma's womb, a suitcase whose lock sprang,
spilled you somewhere in Europe, Hannah,
to join the flight from Mother Russia.
Adele, then I, were born
in a cramped corner of the diaspora,
this side of Ellis Island,
too late to suit Poppa.

I see you, Hannah,
float under yellowed, peeled ceilings,
from stove to sink, dresser to bed,
room to room, dodging our father,
who dealt anger as if there was profit in it.
He did not speak to you for years.
What was your sin that outlived each *Yom Kippur?*

You moved between our mother's shuffled shadows,
rounded the reaches of her voice.
You outflanked our middle sister
who sliced the air with her shrieks.
Your features shifted as often as clouds.
For each of us you molded a face.

Before swastikas unfurled in Prague, before Dachau,
I remember your porcelain fingers
on the Victrola's *Z*-shaped crank.
We listened to Caruso sing
La donna è mobile from *Rigolleto.*

You tuned my ears to Mozart;
guided my eyes to Klee and Kandinsky;
helped me imagine Christopher Wren's spires,
Koyota's gongs resounding in wooden temples,
Versailles's mirrored crystal,
the Taj Mahal's reflections,
the jungle strangling Ankor Wat.

Between Friday fish and Sunday wafers, Dominic,
the club boxer from the Bronx,
courted you for months with roses,
from which he'd trimmed the thorns, and whispers
translucent as moth wings brushing light.
He showed me how to fight,
taught me dominoes and rummy.

Instead, you stood beneath a wedding *chuppah* with Sol,
a bearded *Chasid,* a garment cutter,
with curled *peyas* tucked behind his ears.
From that day, a storm buffeted the two of you
beneath mattresses, under tables,
in sealed boxes of *Pesachdikah* glass dishes
stored in high cupboards.
Did you marry him for happiness or penance?
Did you choose Sol, over Dominic, the *shegetz,*
to buy back Poppa's love?

But Poppa spent your wedding day
delivering wet wash to his customers.
Before the next winter clenched its teeth,
Poppa flew south like a gander, dragging Momma with him.
They never came back.

Hannah, what did you give, what did you withhold?
You never bore me a niece to rock.
You never gave Sol a son to ransom from the rabbi
at a *pidyon haben,* with a silver *shekel,*
a son who would recall his father's failed name
each year at *Yizkor.*

All Sol gave you was loose change,
doled out on an installment plan.
In the twelfth year of your marriage,
the fiftieth of his life, he died;
left you only *yahrzeit* candles
to measure out your burned-down years.

Now that my years are scattered pebbles,
I wake nights awash in darkness
and you're there, Hannah, but for the bones.

YAHRZEIT: DEATH'S ANNIVERSARY DREAM

Last night, my father
stood naked like me:

His penis, smaller than I'd imagined,
his chest indented like a battered suitcase.
An asterisk of saber scars
engraved on his stomach pogroms he'd survived.
No tailor had altered
his fretted skin to fit.

To his left, two paces back,
her clothes heaped like plucked feathers
of a *Shabbas* chicken,
my mother stood on feet
poured without a mold,
bound up in veins.
Her breasts, puffed out gray poached eggs.
Her pubic hair twined like brambles
beneath belly folds for each child.

All their years recorded.

When I saw them,
I covered my groin with both hands.
They covered their mouths.

THE DEAD

Here's a book a dead man wrote.
There blooms a wild rosebush
transplanted by your grandmother
before you were conceived.

The dead are strewn leaves,
wicks without wax,
waves that have ebbed,
fallen stars.
They are what was.

Bury them.

PUSSAN, 1951

From a hilltop
north of the harbor,
I watched beside a Swedish nurse
the ascending moon blanch and contract.
We pulled dried octopus skin between clenched teeth,
drank sake from clay jars,
let our bodies thresh the stubbled incline.

On the way back in a borrowed jeep,
sniper fire riddled the radiator,
spare tire, the nurse's blue knapsack-purse.
Five miles down the road,
to get us back behind friendly lines,
I pissed in the radiator,
dry as a picked-over bone.

AT THE BEACH

I let my son
bury me in sand.
His mother kneels to help,
joins in laughter.

Tall as a crab,
my eyes rivet the horizon.
My tongue is a tiny flag
flicking thirst.

I study shattered shells,
count feet and candy wrappers.
A breeze shifts
the grains of my grave.

ARTHUR BRYANT'S BARBEQUE

Each time I order burned ends,
my thoughts turn to Leviticus,
the priests,
the temple offerings.

HEART'S CONCEIT:
REFLECTIONS DURING DIASTASIS

All is well.
My heart experiences blood: it is
blood's metronome, enunciator,
blood's inner sanctum;
it floats a bloodbath,
suckles blood, expectorates.

Jockeyed by adrenaline,
gentled by sleep,
my heart engages in constant commerce
with lungs, liver, kidneys, spleen;
it accommodates
and is accommodated
in return.

Cyclical percussionist
inside an echo chamber,
my heart seizes each pulse,
flexes its muscle, makes a fist;
telegraphs its message,
scribbles its mysteries on graphs.

EACH TRIP

for JW

I invent longing
as if it were new,
watch the sky
for her plane to fall
into my pitted glove.

I dream the soles of her feet,
the down tracing her lower spine,
the way she sings my name
in morning's frost,
evening's fire.

GLOSSARY OF HEBREW AND YIDDISH WORDS
(in order of appearance)

25 **Shema:** Literally means "listen";
designates a prayer consisting of six words
which proclaims the One God. Observant Jews
recite the *Shema* when they are close to death.

27 **Torah:** Commonly referred to by Christians
as the *Pentateuch,* the first five books
of the *Old* Testament..

27 **Simchat Torah:** Annual holiday
celebrates the "joy of *Torah.*"

41 **golem:** In East European Yiddish folklore,
rabbis versed in cabalistic wisdom,
such as Rabbi Low of sixteenth-century Prague,
infused life into these difficult to control creatures
in order to protect Jews during times of danger.
In my poem, the building blocks employed
by Dr. Frankenstein substitute
for the clay the rabbis used.

41 **minyan:** A quorum of no less than ten adult
Jewish males who gather for worship.

51 **shul:** A synagogue.

51 **cheder:** An elementary level school
for Orthodox Jewish boys.

52 **Yom Kippur:** Jews' holiest fast day,
the *Day of Atonement.*

53 **chuppah:** A canopy, which traditionally consists of a fringed prayer shawl or *tallis,* beneath which a bride and groom take their matrimonial vows.

53 **Chasid:** A member of an ultra-orthodox East European Jewish sect.

53 **peyas:** Long sideburns. Ultra-orthodox Jews believe that the *Torah* forbids men to cut or shave their facial hair.

53 **Pesachdikah:** The designation for foods and other items approved for the Jewish Passover holiday. *Seder* means "order" and refers to the traditional sequence of prayers, recitations and partaking of symbolic foods and wine. The *Last Supper* observed by Jesus and his disciples was a Passover *seder.*

53 **shegetz:** A gentile male.

54 **pidyon haben:** A symbolic ritual that exempts first born sons from serving the priesthood. It dates back to King Solomon's temple.

54 **shekel:** An Israeli coin which originated in biblical times.

54 **Yizkor:** A prayer which memorializes the dead.

54 **yahrzeit:** The anniversary of a death.

55 **Shabbas:** Jews observe the sabbath from sundown on Friday until sundown on Saturday. Chicken is one of the traditional entrees.

Thomas Zvi Wilson

was born in New York City,
moved to Arkansas in his early forties
and Kansas when he was fifty.
He is a painter and sculptor
with fourteen one-person exhibits to his credit,
including seven in Manhattan galleries.
His work is represented
in twenty-five museum and university collections,
and he has completed a number
of public sculpture and mural commissions.

He is married to Jeanie Wilson,
an educator, poet, and short story writer.
His son Josh lives in New York City.